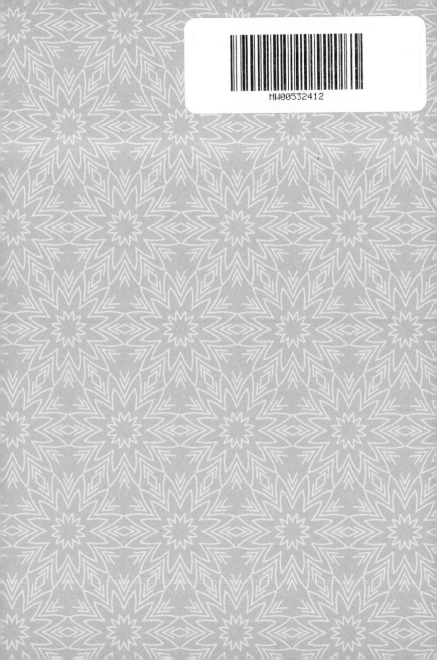

To:

_____

From:

_____

Date:

_____

Visit Christian Art Gifts website at www.christianartgifts.com.

Blessings for a #1 Teacher

© 2012
First edition 2012 by Christian Art Gifts, RSA
Second edition 2016 by Christian Art Gifts, RSA
Third edition 2022 by Christian Art Gifts, USA

Designed by Allison Sowers

Images used under license from Shutterstock.com

ISBN 978-1-64272-393-9

Printed in China

28 27 26 25 24 23
10 9 8 7 6 5 4 3 2 1

BLESSINGS
FOR A GREAT
Teacher

Christian art gifts

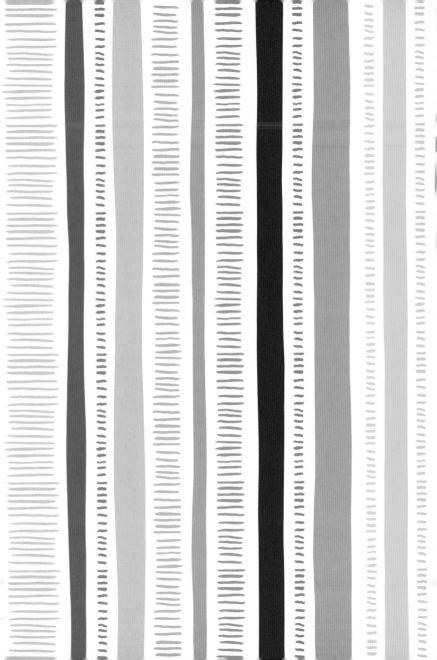

Teacher's Prayer

Lord, please help me
to strengthen their
voices, bodies & minds,
to express their feelings &
control them sometimes.
To explore what's near
& venture afar,
but most important
to love who they are.

- ANONYMOUS -

You're a **special** person!
A teacher who truly **cares**.
Know that you're **appreciated**,
and **daily** in my prayers.

- KARLA DORNACHER -

He shall **give** His angels
charge over you, to keep
you in all your **ways**.

- PSALM 91:11 -

Be of good **courage**, and He
shall **strengthen** your heart,
all you who **hope** in the LORD.

- PSALM 31:24 -

An apple lasts a short
time in the hand of a teacher.
A bit of *wisdom* lasts a
lifetime in the mind
of a child.

Your love has given me great joy & encouragement.

- PHILEMON 7 -

Time spent with children is never wasted.

- ANONYMOUS -

Commit to the LORD whatever you do, and your plans will succeed.

- PROVERBS 16:3 -

Every child
is a bundle
of potential
& promise.

- ANONYMOUS -

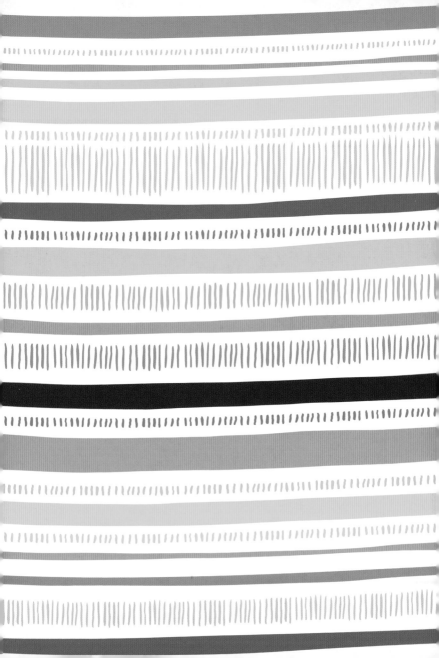

School is a building that has four walls — with tomorrow inside. - LON WATTERS -

Wisdom is more precious than rubies. - PROVERBS 8:11 -

Love is a great teacher. - ST. AUGUSTINE -

In matters of style, swim with the current. In matters of principle, stand like a rock. - THOMAS JEFFERSON -

Love is a better teacher than duty. - ALBERT EINSTEIN -

You make a difference!

Do all the *good* you can,
by all the *means* you can,
in all the *ways* you can,
in all the *places* you can,
to all the *people* you can,
as long as you ever can.

- JOHN WESLEY -

*All our children
deserve teachers who
believe they can
learn and who will
not be satisfied
until they do.*

- JOE NATHAN -

To teach, to guide, to explain, to help, to nurture – these are life's noblest attainments.

- FRANK TYGER -

We are God's workmanship, created in Christ Jesus *to do good works,* which God prepared in advance for us to do.

- EPHESIANS 2:10 -

*Kites rise
highest against the
wind, not with it.*

- WINSTON CHURCHILL -

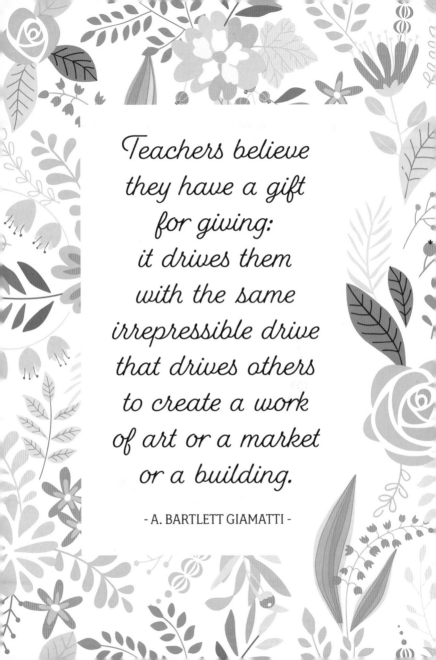

Teachers believe
they have a gift
for giving:
it drives them
with the same
irrepressible drive
that drives others
to create a work
of art or a market
or a building.

- A. BARTLETT GIAMATTI -

Train up a child in the
way he should go, and
when he is old he will
not turn from it.

- PROVERBS 22:6 -

I will instruct you and
teach you in the way
you should go; I will
counsel you with My
loving eye on you.

- PSALM 32:8 -

Seven days

without PRAYER

makes one weak.

- ALLEN E. BARTLETT -

He who
opens a school door,
closes a prison.

- VICTOR HUGO -

An Apple a Day

A Recipe for an excellent teacher:

A is for aptitude – intelligence to teach

P is for patience – when they're hard to reach

P is for prayer – when my day's work is done

L is for love – may I love everyone

E is for empathy – a feeling heart.

Mix them together –
and now we can start.

- MELODY CARLSON -

I have not stopped
giving thanks for
you, remembering
you in my prayers.

- EPHESIANS 1:16 -

Children are messengers we send to a time we will not see.

- ANONYMOUS -

Teaching kids
to count is fine,
but teaching them
what counts is best.

- BOB TALBERT -

Shine as lights among the people of this world, as you hold firmly to the message that gives life.

- PHILIPPIANS 2:15-16 -

To teach is
to learn twice.

- JOSEPH JOUBERT -

Whatever your hand
finds to do, do it
with all your might.

- ECCLESIASTES 9:10 -

A teacher affects
eternity; he can
never tell where his
influence stops.

- HENRY ADAMS -

Wisdom will enter
your heart, and
knowledge will be
pleasant to your soul.

- PROVERBS 2:10 -

Whatever you do,
work at it with
all your heart,
as working for
the Lord, not for
human masters.

- COLOSSIANS 3:23 -

A good teacher remembers what it was like to be taught by their favorite teacher.

- ROBERT MCLAIN -

Blessed is the hand that prepares a pleasure for a child, for there is no saying when and where it may bloom forth.

- DOUGLAS WILLIAM JERROLD -

Be faithful in small things
because it is in them that
your strength lies.

- MOTHER TERESA -

God regards with how
much love a person
performs a work, rather
than how much he does.

- THOMAS À KEMPIS -

Do not be conformed
to this world, but be
transformed by
the renewing of your
mind, that you may
prove what is that good
and acceptable and
perfect will of God.

- ROMANS 12:2 -

In my lifetime
I hope to develop ...
Arms that are strong,
Hands that are gentle,
Ears that will listen,
Eyes that are kind,
A mind full of wisdom,
A heart that understands,
A tongue that will
speak softly.

- ANONYMOUS -

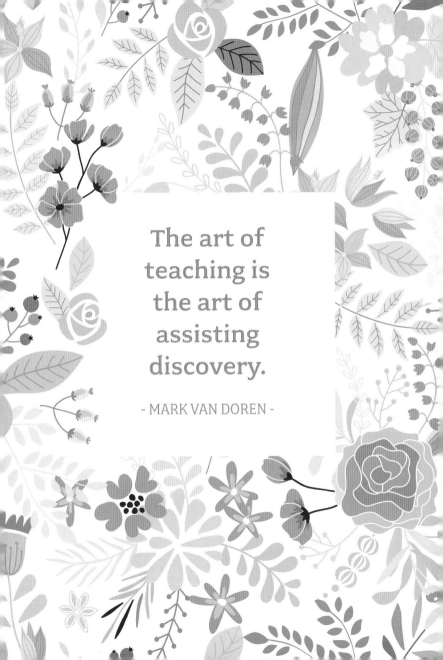

The art of
teaching is
the art of
assisting
discovery.

- MARK VAN DOREN -

If I can put
one touch of

Rosy Sunset

into the life of any
man or woman,
I shall feel that I have
worked with God.

- JOHN MACDONALD -

You have a
special place
in my heart.

- PHILIPPIANS 1:7 -

The best teachers
teach from the heart,
not from books.

- ANONYMOUS -

Every time I think of you, I give thanks to my God.

- PHILIPPIANS 1:3 -

People don't care how much you know until they know how much you care.

- ANONYMOUS -

Kind words can be short and easy to speak, but their echoes are truly endless.

- MOTHER TERESA -

Great works
are performed not
by strength, but
by perseverance.

- SAMUEL JOHNSON -

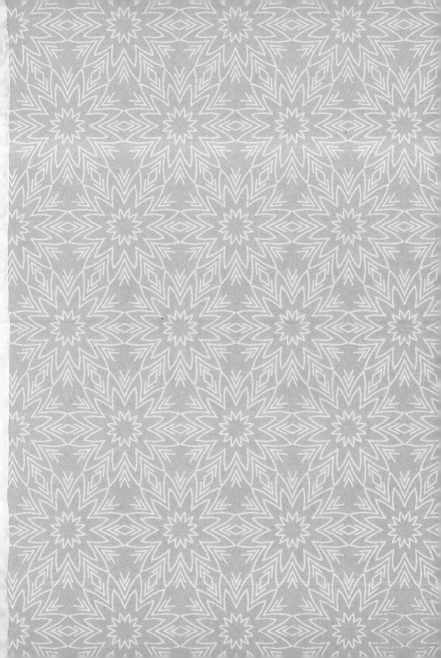

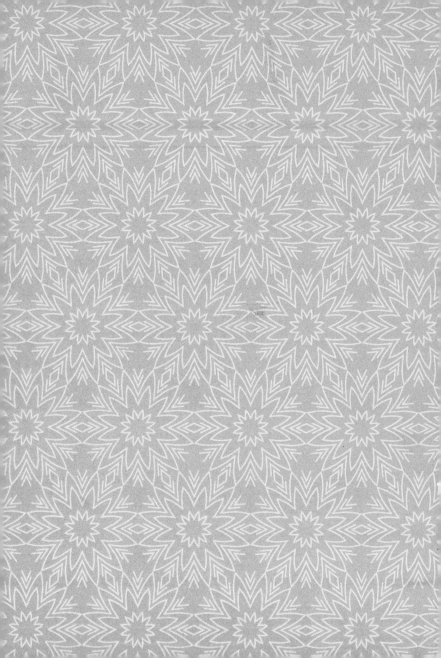